My Father's House

Keith DeClerck

Copyright © 2007 by Keith DeClerck

My Father's House
by Keith DeClerck

Printed in the United States of America

ISBN 978-1-60477-102-2

All rights reserved solely by the author. The author guarantees all contents are original and do not infringe upon the legal rights of any other person or work. No part of this book may be reproduced in any form without the permission of the author. The views expressed in this book are not necessarily those of the publisher.

Unless otherwise indicated, Bible quotations are taken from the Spirit Filled Life™ Bible for Students, New King James Version of the Bible, Copyright © 1995 by Thomas Nelson, Inc.

www.xulonpress.com

Bert & Shirley,

There are not enough words in this book to describe how we feel about you both. It is like God has given us our own personal angels to walk this journey with us.

We love ya.

Keith & Carin

Dedication

My Father's House is dedicated to my Heavenly Father whose love for me is so great that He has never given up on me, even when I had given up on myself; and to my earthly father whose love of words and lyrics and poem and song taught me to feel deep within, yet whose love for my mother taught me to set my heart free.

Acknowledgements

I would like to thank LJP and Reality Ministries for making this collection of my work possible; my brother Richard whose support and guidance has been steadfast and true throughout the years; and my wife Carin, whom God placed in my life at just the critical moment as if an angel had been sent to block the furnace door.

My Father's House

Psalm 139: 4 For there is not a word on my tongue, But behold, O Lord, You know it altogether.

Contents

I
Newborn Son 14
Race Day..15
Under a Sheltered Sky 18
Tomorrow's Gold 19
To Know Love 20
This Life Escapes Me..21
Sanctuary Heart...22
Prayer Mine...23
Dreamer's Weld 24
Cradle Against the Door..25
Caught in the Ripple 28
Center of My Desire..29

II
My Father's House..32
I Can Remember 34
For the Love of a Son..36
For the Love of a Daughter...39
Against All Odds...41
Word..43
On Being Ten 45
Master Plan 47
Between the Moon and Me 48
The Question...49

III
On Wings of Angels 52
Freedom 53
The Promise 55
Oh Valentine 56
New Leaf 57
One in Age 58
God's Grace 59
Beyond My Understanding 60
Always and Forever 61
Johna's Song 62
Ari Nui and the Green Flash 63
Mary's Song 65
In Her Eyes 68

IV
Teacher's Café 72

I

Psalm 51:6 Behold, You desire truth in the inward parts, And in the hidden part You will make me to know wisdom.

Newborn Son

In my torturous thoughts
Knives wielded by warriors from the past
I forget the truth, and dwell on demons
Yet like a river, Your spirit flows through me
Eyes welled in pain, red as torn flesh
You have seen more than enough
Yet You say, "Place a finger in My wound,
Never doubt that I am real."

For Your love is the strength of nations
Your omniscience a scalpel refined
With each incision You flay the fearful skin
Stripping away the chains that bind my esteem
Lifting my countenance to shoulder the weight
In Your grace, my heart, an eagle soars
In my faith I find a foothold to rise up
You've pulled me from the quicksand, plucked a thorn from the earth.

Hence I will no longer doubt Your existence
Nor wonder at my purpose, Lord
For through You I can forge eternity
So find me Lord in prayer
Call my name out loud in the dark
Point Your mighty finger to guide me
Laying my heart wide open for all the world to see
Praying in my nakedness, You have given life, Your newborn son.

Race Day

Death and destruction grew from my back as a tree,
Rooted in the bitterness that welled inside me,
Its weight hunching me over in sorrow and self-pity,
Muscles ridged with fear, the bark that enveloped my soul.

The vile harvest, its rotten fruit littered the plain of my existence,
My neck was stiff with inadequacy, the cold touch of the devil's hand,
He thrived on my weakness, stripped my heart naked with his cunning,
Left an anvil of sin crushing down upon my shoulders.

He sent his minions to shout in my face,
Their lies licking at my ears,
Feel the curve of the concubine hip, they'd say,
Taste the sweet forgiveness of alcohol and pills.

Fruit of lust, fruit of anger, fruit of rebellion,
Feeding on the poison that cumulates in the soil,
I cursed myself, the only thing I could do well was sin,
Embracing the deception, like a child holds onto a mother's arm.

Athletic potential deprived of a finish line,
Marriage driven to the dead-ends of divorce,
Intellect succumbed to the power of Pharmacia,
While despair raged in my chest, for I knew not who I was.

Somehow Truth found me no matter where I hid
Persistent in love, He wanted me for His own,
Gaining a foothold in His promise, I wanted to run the race,
But my legs had atrophied in the darkness.

He carried the burden of my sin—past, present, future,
As I healed, gently guiding me up the pinnacle to forgiveness,

My Father's House

I approached with anticipation, enthusiasm, apprehension,
A journey down a path that evaporates behind my step.

Can there be such a place for me?
Where barriers are destroyed, bewilderment leads to joy,
Though dark forces tried to mire me in confusion,
I wanted to fight for my freedom.

In this place, they came bludgeoned by humanity,
As me, their torsos once twisted in the smoke of hell fires,
Standing tall like wheat four hundred acres strong,
Their heads facing the heavens to soak in His reign.

I clasped my wife's hand, the love she has for me,
As we stood beside each other in this earthquake of passion,
Younger than I, but stronger still, their joy surged through us and around us,
Such extravagance for the King I had never seen.

Runners were gathering at the gun, athletes trained in praise,
Awaiting the percussion of angels to begin their marathon of Truth,
Race Day—the Lord welling out from this place of worship,
So prolific, the earth to be enveloped in His glory.

And from the thunder came the two for Christ
"Time to lace up your shoes for Jesus," they said,
Sent from above to secure the way,
The steel of my commitment to be forged.

They were the instruments of His love,
The probe and scalpel he would use to search my heart, my soul,
To flay away the festering sickness, and tear
At the roots of bitterness that bound my purpose.

Humility was their strength, Faith their shield,
Wisdom imparted from God to journey into the core of my mortality,

Releasing me, one by one, from the demons of my life, my death,
Love for a stranger without reservation, warm as the morning sun.

As demons scattered like cockroaches in the Light
Shaking from the battle, my body bent, a reed of exhaustion,
Witchcraft and paranoia caved my legs, heaved and writhed under my skin,
Fearing the final judgment, they fought on with impudence.

The two brought in specialists to massage my heart,
Pump God's lifeblood back into my veins,
Their ferocious calls on the Lord, powerful and decisive,
Finally breaking the last vestige of the demons' hold.

Then it was done, God had severed the ties
To generation, to death and destruction,
The tree fell from my back unceremoniously,
As I lifted my head to a new horizon.

Today standing in the sun of my Father's love,
Surrounded by the gifts that flow from His grace,
I feel illuminated, eradicated, redeemed in His name,
For if the Lord is with me who can be against me.

Jesus was the first to run the race, made man
He fought the demons' shout unto the cross to save me,
So how much shall I endure to return Him that love?
I know now never as much as He deserves.

Forever I will remember this day of blessing,
Those people who in God toppled the tree from my back,
And I will run the race, no matter the distance,
For it's Race Day--relentless unto the finish line.

Under a Sheltered Sky

Under a sheltered sky
We as children lay our heads
Embraced in a wrap of comfort
Caught in a time-spun web.
For in God's fervent touch
True blessings brought ten-fold
He graced us with his favorite gift
A wonder ancient, never old.

Sure deep is the eternal ocean
Wide is the crescent universe
Vast is thy fruitful imagination
Immortal is the spoken verse.
Yet cast in the balance of fortune
Weighed against this godsend true
All shrink empty into cold oblivion
Compared to my love of you.

Tomorrow's Gold

Have you ever been on a drunken weep
Where life is short and emotions sweet
Strong cord heart, mind of courage
Feelings scarred
Deep as a river, clear as a shout
Tear my paper skin hands of the roiling tide
What was is no more, what is to be
Flashes gold tomorrow
Slivers to my eye, staves to my soul
Loneliness intense calls the gathering gloom as insects to the feast
I am but a myth unto myself
A wish to soar into the spectral light.

To Know Love

Bleeding the page
Hope and sorrow mingle red
To be all to one, a dream
Heaven sent in angel's arms.

Twist as smoke
Roots grasp the passion earth
Harden oak to stand the storm
Shade the grass blue, cool day.

To know love past the cordon life
Last breath sweet as cherry
Visions painted on a canvas soul
Carry me forever.

This Life Escapes Me

The sun is finally breaking,
Driving out the last tears from the sky,
While orange hues of morning,
Break across the crown of trees.
The colors radiate Your glory,
There is solace in this place.
I hear the waves crashing white on the rocks,
As the struggle of men surround me,
Yet here I find Your love and peace,
Feel the whispery wind of angels' wings.
For I am home in Your presence, unfettered
Sensing with each breath, this life escapes me.

Sanctuary Heart

When the breath escapes you,
When the void chill of night
Settles deep into your bones,
Lay hold of the Sanctuary Heart,
For in its gold lies the strength to go on.

When infirmity plagues you,
When words spoken callously,
Cut layers through your skin,
Lay hold of the Sanctuary Heart
For in its shape lies the love to go on.

When darkness circles 'round you,
When the looming past closes in,
To rob you of the glories ahead,
Lay hold on the Sanctuary Heart,
For in its spirit lies the forgiveness to go on.

When the future scares you,
When the weight of the world,
Crushes down upon your shoulders,
Lay hold of the Sanctuary heart,
For in your Father lies the answer to go on.

When you wear this heart,
Remember that I love you,
That without you my life would be distraught,
That you mean more to me than any earthly thing,
That even though my days are of certain numbers,
That I will always remember the one night,
When we met, and the soft touch of your dress.

Prayer Mine

Find me Lord in prayer
Call my name in the dark
Point a finger to guide me
Iron the curves from my life
Take my heart and run.

For if all that I am is dust
Random wisps of cosmic air
I would have no purpose
Yet I feel a greater hand
At work in my mind.

Blessed by You I am your instrument
Let me spread Your joy with my pen
Grip the core of man's breath
Burn as fire bright in the soul
Of those You touch by me.

Dreamer's Weld

I am cast in a dreamer's weld
I must express my heart.
There is no part of me that can exist
Without the deepest cut.

You are the epitome of all that is me
I must strike the pen to the page.
I was put here to take purpose
To inspire someone, if only one.

God gave me the craving
He has blessed me so.
I will touch those naked and dark
Shed emotion into the cracks of life.

Be my anchor, be my flow
My passion was sent by Him.
Let me share it with you
There is so much to know.

Cradle Against the Door

Trapped in a chamber of my own design,
The winter snow, the fetus lies steaming.
My fetus in a barrel by the barn.

Dreadful winter.
The logs of my cabin sweat with foul humidity,
Burning flesh of my soul, branded
While the blood of new life escapes the steel confines
Into breathless vapor.

Here is my cradle against the door,
Once made for a baby's coos, now
Stopping the Lord from coming in.
Freedom so sought after, lost
To another lie.

Truth be it: The choice before passion,
Not after the miracle has begun.
I am such a fool: My burden
Is lessened by this act?
What course of mankind will I travel
For self indulgence?
Can I rationalize my baby is now in a better place?
Did I prepare the hummingbird in its struggle to fly?
Did I form the ocean to be the hub in the spokes of life?
What then prepared me for this decision?
My knowledge of the future?

My heart is torn with incompletion.
My chest filled with liquid rage.
I weep until my eyes are red . . .
Red with the blood of my unborn children.

Dare I say: "To be human
Is to be made in the image of God,"

My Father's House

For love be at our center, if not,
Only evil remains, and love has left me today.

I have let the voices toll
My future: "Humanity over God,"
As I ventured headlong from the truth,
Deceived into thinking,
I should have no part in God, as if
I was my own creation.

With each lick of my ears, the sorghum sound, the lies
Flowed like water from his mouth,
Slowly the weight countered,
Wheels turned reason against reason,
My soul like grist in the devil's mill.

Oh, but my disgust is in vain.
All that is left now is the empty shell,
Hollow with sorrow and shame,
Freedom of choice chained by guilt.

I cannot deny it,
A piece of me has left today never to return,
A piece of my soul sent without me to wait.
Shall I stack another cradle by the door?
The fruit of another lover to block the entrance.
Shall I grease the porch with hurry, or opiates,
To keep the Truth at bay?
Or replace the locks with keys from some other
More calculating god, the tally of eternal atonement
Grinding false notches on its shank.

No, I am trapped inside this cabin of guilt
By my own design, until
I can push aside my imperfection
With hands of grace.
In my mind's eye I see,

Each day I wait, bitterness will salt my wound, until
I am but a festering sore of the woman
That was once Eve.

I must fling the door wide open, infernal heat escape,
Before there is time for confusion to rear his ugly head.
Before it's too late, let the forgiveness of Spring replace
The temporal lust that wintered my heart.
Be quick!
Let Him, who first charted the universe, replenish my soul
With His warm caress, the sweet taste of my eternal lover
On my lips as I bid him a bow to come in.

Caught in the Ripple

Crouched in the middle of a stream
Unbeknown of the future
Caught in the ripple
Cool waters tickle my toes
Smile face at the wonder
Risen from the ashes
Spirit soar above the mountains
Spy down the valleys
For love has come from vapor
Breath of God
And it takes me to the ends of the earth.

Center of My Desire

The trees in leaf as the days grow long to summer.
The ever-changing canvas He paints over my head.
The flit of sparrow as it darts from limb to tree.
The call of the Meadowlark in search of food.

In that place where time and space cease to exist,
Where love is the only dimension, and joy
The measure of our days.

He calls to me in the morning,
Bright shower of gifts for the day.
He waits at the edge of the meadow,
The tree line the perimeter of His court,
And there in this quiet place, He charts
The compass of my day.

II

Psalm 8: 4 What is man that You are mindful of him, And the son of man that You visit him?

My Father's House

Last night I stood outside my father's house,
Dark curtain sky filled with pinhole lights,
The frozen air cracked with hard work,
I knew he was near.

Leather smell of boots toiled and rough,
Whine of blades, the sawdust swirls,
Marveling at the labor of his hands,
His voice grew bright in my ear.

I felt the warmth of his breath,
Clear like dew on summer grass,
The winter night shuddered at his laugh,
As the vision came all so clear.

Arms raised to the heavens, he stood in ageless youth,
Eyes blue-crystal filled with delight,
The eyes I knew as a child,
Those days we walked the forest path.

Through the iron of heaven's gate,
His voice lifted like a swell in my throat,
I could feel his thought upon me,
Knew his love place a thumb to my heart.

Count the stars in the eastern sky, he said,
Then the west, the north, at last south,
Watch the flowers bloom and fade the day,
Follow the composer as he circles his wand.

In the eyes of the unknowing,
Eternity looms lonely as the horizon,
A wave on the endless ocean,
Wandering lost along a serpentine trail.

My Father's House

But I tell you I have seen the Truth,
The Light has stripped away the darkness,
My struggle there was but a dream,
Looking back I marvel at the inconsequence.

Furrowed with valleys the earth takes prisoners,
Listen with your heart, see with your soul,
Find the mountaintops and spy down the abyss,
Watchful of the steps slick with ice.

Constant as the rising sun,
Solemn as the morning forest,
Unwavering as a river bent on the sea, he was,
And I ran, his son, from his ways.

Yet now I see his eyes in my mirror,
I hear his words in my voice,
He is in me, and I in him,
Strangely more the same.

Last night I stood outside my father's house,
Heard the echo of my sorrow fade,
Then with a flutter I felt a throb in my heart,
That I knew he left for me.

I Can Remember

I can remember as a child growing up in a big old house in the country,
With a narrow front porch, and stairs that creaked every time you tried to sneak.
And my Aunt Mary and Uncle George bless their hearts,
Who had none but took me for their very own.
I can remember the smell of cookies in the kitchen while I took a nap, boiling coffee,
The sound of the sprinkler outside my summer window, whirling out its rainbows across the lawn;
The click of the oscillating fan blowing its coolness across my face, a twist of fresh cut grass on the wind.

As a child in this place I remember too untying Dad's leather boots when he got home from work.
The enormous hug, the barrel chest, stretching my arms to barely touch my fingertips at his back.
The smell of sawdust on his clothes, the blue in his eyes.
Or sitting at mom's feet while she embroidered pillow cases,
Her taking a moment to run a finger through my hair.
The sound of her jewelry box playing Oklahoma.
The warm, safe feel of her apron against my cheek.

Life has always been mottled like the sun through the trees,
Shifting patterns of light and dark against the ground.
The footpath we must walk, the soil slick beneath our feet.
Not always two steps forward, but one-step back.

Yet even though I have wandered in the dark, and the dark has wandered over me,
My parents always have encouraged me to live in the light.
The glass half full, not half empty.
No matter the storm they were always there to tie up to, anchors.
So I guess what I want to say to them now is that: "Home was a great place to grow up."

Should all children be so lucky.
Those times I said, "I want to blow this hole," were just the ramblings of idle youth.

For the Love of a Son

Hollow is my heart
I shout but the echoes desert me
Like a rock falling into a deep well
The splash is so quiet
It may have been tears

You are the arm
That has been severed
The leg that atrophied
In the dark
While you were taken away

You are part of me
Yet not part of me
You are here
Yet you are not here
A myth born of me

Like a ghost
I feel you
Shiver on my spine
Your breath
Whispery like rain

I wish I could hug you
I wish I could hold you
I wish I could smell
Then rustle your hair
Now, not later

I pray to the Lord
Everyday
That you are the better parts of me
That you will grow and know
I am with you

As I cannot at times
God has put His arms
Around you
For me
And watched over you

I pray he has told you
The good things about me
That you will feel it in your chest
Like a gasp
When you see me

All those nights
When you went to bed alone
And I wasn't there
Understand
I was thinking of you

Your name
Branded on my heart
I will take to my grave
For you are mine
No other's

Imagine
Hollow as a well
Imagine that in your chest
The nothingness
The void

Cold and darkness
Surround you
A rock may fall
To the bottom
I have been

Love
Sucked away
Like so much blood
Sucked from my heart
Never from my soul

For the way you roll your eyes
The way you giggle and laugh
The way your ticklish on the ribs
The way you fight me at bedtime
I love all those things

The way you're so scared
To try new things
Yet once bitten, no looking back
Taking it with all the fury
That God has put within you

I am proud of the way
You love to read
I am proud of the way
You love to be precise
That's you

I am proud of the way
You take such joy in little things
Orange kitties
Patrick and Spongebob
Playing basketball

Praising God as you do
Perfect childish way
Riding your bike
The nature park where we run
And see beavers and birds

For the Love of a Daughter

My love for you, daughter, is without question,
Deep as the ocean and wide as the sky,
Emerging at birth, a seedling rooted in my soul,
Intricate yet strong, to flower for eternity.

I remember the first step, the first cry,
The first utterance of my name,
The way you curled upon my chest,
Your breath light upon my neck.

When the quiet of morning gave promise,
When the solace of evening echoed the day,
I found wonder in your perfection,
The smell of innocence in your hair.

God had given me a gift in the midst of despair,
A treasure to be protected beyond my own life.
I took to the duty with fervor it seemed,
Poured out my love in endless streams of emotion.

Yet as a bolt of lightning splits the sky,
There was a crack in the plate of my existence.
Brought there by the first fallen heroes,
The fist of God angry upon their hearts.

No matter how carefully I washed it,
Or placed it on the shelf, the crack grew,
Splintering into veins of failure and disappointment,
Unaffected by the glue of my prideful will.

I could not change it, I cannot still
It is beyond my power to heal the shards.
But if my love cannot mend it, so great as it is for you,
Who then or what then can be the salve?

My Father's House

In this world, no greater love exists or endures,
This father to his child, yet I have failed you.
So true to my mind, a tear at my heart, how can it be?
Not out of malice, nor rejection, but love?

See true love is imperfect in this place, impossible to attain.
Though sonnets profess it, and our lips so easily proclaim it,
Love is strangled by mortal ambition, left untarnished
Only in the minds of poets and fools and schoolgirls with trusting smiles.

Therefore I give you back to God from whence you came,
Not discarded--oh child hear my heart as it bleeds the page,
But alive in the hope that only His love can secure.
For I am limited in my virtue, He is limitless in His grace.

Make no doubt, I will always be your father, here
To love you with the full extent of my heart,
But compared to me, His house is filled with ageless wonders.
The universe is His footstool, and He has called you to His throne.

So place your love for Him above all others,
Just as He loved you first before you were mine.
The agony He endured was so that you would not have to
For the love of a daughter--He gave His life.

Against All Odds

Stare at the horizon and imagine sixty years
How the porcelain blue of heaven, finds the rooted brown of earth
How together they are married
From their union the world was birth.

Such as it was, for both man and wife
She of porcelain, fragile, yet constant still
He of rooted earth, simple, solid, provider
Their marriage a mingling of wills.

So take a moment to wonder
Let your thoughts be focused with mine
See the depth of this day before us
Their accomplishment beyond our time.

Bitter cold; hail from a Midwestern sky
Land that spewed rocks in the spring
Money scarce as dust in the wind
No count for a diamond ring.

Labor endless as the ocean tide
From morning till night, hard times
Through sickness, and wars, and presidents
Yet against all odds they survived.

And we wonder at the ability, the commitment, the strength
To weather six children in stride
Today we see two as a heroic feat
Now wonder how many nights they cried.

God laid plans for their life in the beginning
As a smith, hammered them into gold
Look around you; take a good look at you and me
In your sight their purpose unfolds.

My Father's House

For my father is like a whetstone,
His children sharpened against the grain.
And my mother pliant as the willow tree,
Providing shelter from the rain.

So lest not forget it is because of them
Their faith in the Lord above
No matter what life has prepared for us
We can handle it; we have their love.

Word

I can imagine my Father
Standing on a ridge, in the forest
His suspenders taut on his shoulders
Smell of wood smoke rubbed into his skin.
Though, save for the steel blue of his eyes,
The features of his face have run from my memory.

Together the sound of his voice, which I'd known from birth,
Has since death also faded from my cells, yet today
His words are as clear as the mountain stream
He so enjoyed, and their meaning in my life
As strong as the hands that gripped an axe at fourteen.

I can imagine as well my heavenly Father
Sitting on a throne, in an olive grove
Mankind a leather yoke about his shoulders
Smell of ancient myrrh rubbed into his skin.
Though, save for the steel blue of his eyes,
The features of his face are unimportant to me.

The sound of His voice has never graced my ears,
Though His thoughts appear in my mind sometimes
Without volume, or accent, as a voice might
As clear as if I had said them myself, yet
With sure wisdom I could never muster.

My father wrote some of his words for me to read
Of history, and family, and heritage
None portrayed of brilliance or wisdom, although
They were in my eyes a testimony of courage,
A collection that reconstructed the man.

God's word, His operating instructions without falter,
Authored time and dimension, now after intermission,
Exposing truth without judgment, bringing authority

In a world sick with hopelessness and shame,
A recollection of the construction of men.

On Being Ten

How much fun it was to be down along the creek,
Throwing rocks and watching them disappear
In the lush, or tumble back to earth
From the mossy wall.

To hear the wonderful laughs that he
Would make at each unpredictable fall,
Bounce and splash, joyous eruption
From deep inside his life.

Prodding the newt in the leaves
Along the creek bed, with a stick,
Wondering where his mother was and how cold
His life must be with bugs and rotting leaves
For a bed.

Traveling back to the old rock house, investigating
The cave scribbled with graffiti, scared
By the rubber-winged bat that hangs over the door.

After being at church and reading Proverbs, then off
To NW 23rd, past the horse barns he knew so well
Playing I Spy from the Pizzicato window,
Eating gelato and smelling candles,
Inventing lives for those on the street,
Mysterious black-headed league in the arched window
High above the sidewalk, dressed in black, waiting in black,
Discussions in black.

Throwing rocks at the famous Austin snag – the one
He hit the year before with a mighty bark-chipping blow,
Sending the spider with the white-squiggle-down-its-back
Toward shelter in the arms of a bush.

The size of his hands,
The firmness in his stance,
The sweat atop his forehead,
The color of straw in his hair,
The smell of shampoo lingering there.

It was a perfect day.

Master Plan

Carved into a stone,
At the beginning of time,
God wrote your name,
He placed it next to mine.

How he knew, how he saw,
We will never understand,
Yet the architect of heaven,
Surely had a master plan.

The first day I met you,
I was standing in His grace,
Though I had no premonition,
Of you, and me, this place.

The wonder of that evening,
Today still makes me smile,
I could have done a million things,
And missed you by a mile.

Yet for whatever reason,
We were brought together that day,
You have made me so happy,
I can see no other way.

So remember this always,
With every birthday don't forget,
My love is as deep as the ocean,
Finding you sooner my only regret.

Between the Moon and Me

Between the moon and me
Sets a silver horizon
Trees dressed in shimmer
Water mercurial in the cast
Reach for the ridge
Arms stretched to the promise
No looking back, taking stock
Bright lies the road ribbon
Focus the wind
Heart and soul tendered
Payment due.

The Question

Called out from the New Year's bustle
A voice is heard above the din.
Clear thoughts spoken without tongue
It comes from deep within.

Flicker light as the scene unfolds
Nuzzled shoulders touch first, then hands.
There in the darkened movie palace
A more personal script found plans.

Lively soles kiss the runner's trail
Warm breathe in metronome paces.
Hypnotic beat of peaceful retreat
Eyes speak the words he chases.

Hands held tight race the shopping mall
Serpentine is the crowded course.
Smiles like sunshine warm their face
His mouth poised gathering force.

Now each Sunday as the songs erupt
A mighty passion they evoke.
God graced this woman to his side
He weeps with joy, with love, and hope.

At last in bed at the end of the day
With Bible wide and prayers read.
He can barely hold back his impatient tongue
Rehearsing the words in his tortured head.

For even in the quietest moments
When the lights are turned down low.
And the door is open to the coolness outside
And the dream weaver has begun to sow.

There mingled with the pulse of her love
His heart keeps calling forth her name.
Asking, hoping, longing to say
Four words of timeless fame.

Will you marry me? Will you marry me?
Let the words cry out to the world.
Make me the proudest man alive
Let God's plans for us unfurl.

So say yes, my dear, oh yes
Let your answer sweet as honey be.
Before another minute fades
Say yes, and marry me.

III

Psalm 42:1 As the deer pants for the water brooks, So pants my soul for You, O God.

On Wings of Angels

On wings of angels, wings of saints,
Names written in stone by the finger of God.
Forever may your hearts be united,
May your souls gather as thunder over the firmament,
The roiling sound to shake the earth.
For no greater love has the world yet seen,
Let it prove a shelter from the turmoil of life.

Freedom

Ancient is the story they live
Timeless is the truth they portray
For back in the Garden it was, even then
The same story as today.

He comes forth a son of Adam
Created in the wilderness, a fierce
And brandished heart, as all men
Wild at the core of his being.

She comes forth a daughter of Eve
Created in the image, lush Eden
The crown jewel of His creation
Most intricate flower saved for last.

A man, he has waited for a battle to fight,
Soul longing for an adventure to live.
He has searched his realm through forest and glen,
His eye kept wide for a beauty to rescue.

A woman, she has waited patiently, yearning
To be fought for, longing for an adventure to share.
Within the tower she has concealed
Her riches, her beauty to unveil.

Let not the battle ever be won,
For in the conquest lies the secret of love.

Let not the adventure ever to end,
For in the journey is life, with so much to share.

Let not the rescue ever be thwarted,
For it is in the struggle that beauty reveals.

You were created in the image of God,
Male and female, the traits of His personality
Beyond our imagination, so now you can be one
As He intended, symbols of His majesty.

So take diligence that the roles you were created to live
Are not twisted, forgotten, or left unattended.
For man must fight the battle; woman must be the prize.
Man must lead the adventure; woman must be by his side.
Man must sacrifice for beauty that which woman kindles from deep inside.

In this lies the ultimate freedom
Against the teachings of the world
Against the wandering of the flesh, a future
Bright with love, ripe with commitment, as one
Found in the Garden, walking in the cool of the day.

The Promise

Band of thorns
My heart lies bleeding
Time stretching with anticipation
For absence makes weary the soul
Too few hours in any day to mend
Not like sleep can the loss be caught
Another day

With all my might
I hold the visions
Of days past and futures told
I tremble as a leaf grasping onto Summer heat
For each day with you is sunshine
Each night without
Bitter cold

There is but one promise, our grace, Valentine
Eternity shall hold the key
For in an instant millenniums will pass
Universes shall spawn and fade
Yet year after year our love will never cease
Unfurling like a blossom in our Father's eye
Forever yours

Oh Valentine

Short true is our formal unity
Long lived is our eternal bounds
Ne'er a day goes by in silence
My heart, its love, resounds.

Simple as the enduring water wheel
My mind turns word on word
Grinding love into thoughts on paper
My desire of you to be heard.

For in the universe expanse so great
Only God can put lightning with thunder
And by his hands he formed our love
Like a sculptor the clay bows under.

So hold tight the reins of eternity dear
Ours a stallion rides white in time
Each day in heaven or here on earth
The sun is our chase, Oh Valentine.

New Leaf

As the branches of a tree,
These lives become entwined,
Bony fingers against the forces,
Twisted and shaken in the mind.

Bark flayed naked and left to curl,
Torn from the chest and arm,
Nerves of alder exposed and dark,
Caught in a December storm.

A ray of light from a distant sun,
Warming cold the blood congealed,
Leaves borne of spectral energy,
Mere essence love, strong as steel.

A life renewed in summer heat,
Colors vivid dance and carouse,
Oh how the sunlight flickers in her hair,
Blue eyes crystal grace her smile.

Let there grow a canopy here,
A tent of green where you can lay,
Fresh grass abound to prop your heads,
Cool shade cast blue upon the day.

Words can make the heart sing,
Or bring a country to its knees,
Those spoken without contemplation,
Are as vaporous as the breeze.

Let your vows then become as sword and shield,
Growing feverish in the soul,
True eyes open, bright as embers,
As the leaf, the world unfolds.

One in Age

Years gone by
As if dials spinning in space
What once was bicycles and BB guns
Turned complicated at a furious pace.

Thus this living creation time
Was allowed to contract and expand
Flowing with both joy and desperation
The world slipping through my hands.

Then through you this age became timeless
Life a never-ending surprise
One year waged against eternity
Is zero for sure in my eyes.

This can only happen in an instant
When a three-fold cord is tied
And the here and now is vanquished
Replaced with love endures sublime.

And so my love you are not older than I
For we are one in age it would seem
Joined in our hearts by desires, the truth
A product of our dreams.

Fire flies may ebb and glow the night
Ocean tides will rise and recede
But not my love for you O'dear
Great, true and timeless as the sea.

God's Grace

Never let the sun set on an argument,
Never let the sun rise without an embrace.
Always remember the joy you feel tonight,
For in its strength lies the power of God's grace.

Beyond My Understanding

So this is Christmas
The day Christ became flesh
King of Kings
He held us above the rest.

Three years ago
He changed my life
In an instant
Made it possible, made it right.

A kiss, a smile
A touch of your dress
It took days to realize
His blessing came to rest.

So much has happened
I wonder only at His will
Beyond my understanding
Your love for me still.

Over mountains high
Through the valleys dark
Not a single day
Have you been outside my heart.

So this is Christmas
Give praise to the King
Believe me when I say, my heart
Cries joy when I spy my ring.

Always and Forever

Always
My heart beating in my chest
Blood coursing through my veins
Thoughts clicking the tumblers of my imagination
Summer giving way to Fall
Winter giving way to Spring
The moon tracing the path of the sun
Always I will be with you.

Forever
Beyond our universe, ever expanding in the palm of God
His word, our guideposts to salvation
Love, Hope, Joy, Trust
Souls swollen with the Holy Spirit
Breath of Jesus caught in a newborn's cry
Rushing toward the horizon
Forever I will love you.

Johna's Song

You're beautiful, you're beautiful,
You're beautiful, it's true.
I saw your face in a lonely place,
Sent an angel just for you.

The ocean's deep, the ocean's cold
The ocean's vast, it's true
I know your life can feel the waves
Dark powers want you to.

My love is strong, my love is wide
My love goes on, for thee
So have no fear, you belong to Me
Not swallowed in the sea.

You're beautiful, you're beautiful,
You're beautiful, to Me.
I saw your face in a lovely place,
How life was meant to be.

Ari Nui and the Green Flash

Beyond the horizon, where stories live to be told,
Ari Nui set sail for the curve of the earth,
A pencil-line mystery drawn across his future,
Chapter of life to be written today.

Out from the shore, voices rise and mingle,
Confused, sharp as the cackle of sea birds
Plundering the remnants of dinner, fading
In the wake of ripples in silver words.

Will he come today is the wonder, gazing
At our feet peppered by Abraham's descendants,
Feeling the sun flare and tattoo the skin, women
With the scent of hibiscus lingering in their hair.

The sails of Na Hoku flap yellow-red, billowing
Triangles of wind, as creation divides beneath her hull.
Lazy roll of sea turtle, dolphin dance at her bow,
Invisible reins pulling our carriage through water.

Do you know his whereabouts, Diamond Head,
Or hear the salt sea whispers from watery graves
Singing the lure of the siren songs, barren witness
To ships laden with cargo disappearing in his light.

From where does the wind blow, Ari Nui,
As does our hearts from some unseen force
To carry this vessel across the waves, and rolls,
Whitecaps glistening in the vanishing sun.

Soon the moon will rise gray to blue craters
As echoes of the falling night settle over Waikiki,
Where Tiki torches flicker the stars in a paradise sky,
And dark-skinned beauties sheen the eyes of men.

While Ari Nui stands akimbo at the helm, raven hair,
Shy smile, his old friend Green Flash appears.
Our hearts soar, sun making its escape from the day,
Glint of ray through a crest at the edge of the earth.

Imagine what adventures Ari Nui and the Green Flash await,
Sailing for Indonesian waters, even now, where pirates
Bound in the evening heat, and legends are borne
At midnight from the twist of liars and truth.

Mary's Song

As the sun arose this morning,
I found myself on a mountaintop of Faith,
Gazing down at the wonder of the world,
Rivers and flowers and tumbling surf,
Left only to imagine the Garden and all its splendor.

For in some distant land beyond our recollection,
Treachery and lies have taken us from its view,
Peace and joy to be doled out as commodities,
To be bought and sold, traded for gold,
Left in a world where darkness shades our eyes.

In my younger years, caught in sorrow's grasp,
I entertained the lie, so cleverly disguised,
Thought mine was the only pain to be reconciled,
Convicted the Lord for the injustice in my life,
And searched for heaven where it does not exist.

Raising the hammer high over my head,
I splintered my life into sharp points of agony,
Each blow a remorseful reckoning,
Hope crushed by an iron fist,
Knowing my life was my will, not His.

Slivers of self-pity festered beneath my skin,
I searched for joy in the amber of alcohol,
Peace in the den of chemical addiction,
Pleasure with the charge of lustful eyes,
And abundant anguish followed my days.

I never imagined losing a child as Mary did,
Never thought to look around, to see
From the eyes of another more tested than I,

My Father's House

Her child taken mere hours into breath,
A hole the size of his life left in her heart.

Not once, but twice did she feel this knife,
Slice through her throat of happiness,
While countless others died within her womb,
Her loving arms never to caress,
Her soft voice never to whisper their names.

Hers was not an easy life, blessed with great wealth,
Immune from the curse of crippling disease,
More like a sail in a tempest, yet one constant held true,
Steady today, the same constant that split time in two,
Faith in her Savior, her anchor post of life.

Not as I, when caught in sorrow's grasp,
She found joy in the amber sunrise of creation,
Peace in the folded hands of prayer,
Pleasure in the hearts of children,
Not her own, if there was a difference.

Why shouldn't we place faith in the earth?
Surely the sun will rise and fall each day,
Summer will come after Spring, we've seen.
Yet for many, Eternity looms lonely as a ship,
Disappearing from the horizon on an endless wave.

For Mary, Eternity has come to take her home.
There her crown is filled with many jewels,
Her arms large enough to encompass all her children,
Her love as deep as the ocean still,
For the man she lost, and heaven restored.

Her test here now lies behind her,
The Promise ahead beyond our imagination.
As years melt into moments, true joy and love have come real,

Forever like a blanket to keep her warm,
Savoring the fruit of her life, God's purpose fulfilled.

Basking in the Light of His face,
Like a summer day, He has come to take her.
Almighty, powerful, shining beyond space and time,
Peaceful, loving, a father revered above the earth,
Her lungs have been filled with anticipation.

Throughout her life she set forth with eyes to see,
And ears to hear, she trusted Him as a child.
Why not her reward be so great that our wildest dreams
Are but foolish whims, for where she dines tonight,
Is ridden with love not despair.

So let my prayer today be a simple one,
May God enable us to possess a tiny part of her enduring Faith.
We need not look far to find it, it is there in the strum of our hearts,
For God placed emotion at the center of our chest,
Right where Mary could lead us to discover it.

In Her Eyes

I did not know your mother
As one knows a friend of years
How she would gaze at the fire in a sunset
Or the threat of anger brought her eyes to tears.

She was but an acquaintance after all
A happen stance, a series of turns
In a road that led me here, my loss
Not knowing her before, I learned.

Yet I remember the first time I met her
From the corner of my eye, as if it were etched in glass
Forever in my vision, caught on the canvas of my mind
No solvent could erase her, no alcohol in my grasp.

So there she was, a milestone in my life
Though a jaded memory it must be, a sour wine
For the fear in her eyes stayed with me for days
Like a sickness, viral, unable to cure, only time.

The pain of lost conversation
She sat at the edge wanting in
Not knowing then how to play this game
Her deck cut short, her hand left thin.

Then as the days stretched between us
Facts and reason found it hard to adhere
The torment she endured was reduced to rumor
Again my life, my surroundings, had no fear.

'Til the hands of time came marching
As a clock returns to the beginning of each day
Where soon I found myself confronting the unknown
Having to visit this woman of clay.

So I thought I would find this person
Weak and fragile, conquered, ready to shatter into dust
Like a jar filled with anguish and sorrow
Thrust upon the rocks of God's mistrust.

But alas, my lessons are far from complete
With each breath of life I must learn
For in her eyes the last time we touched
I found peace and love, not spurn.

She smiled and her eyes beat deep in my chest
God was there in this body wracked with ill
Pain and suffering may be eased by drugs
But salvation is free, not a pill.

She had been transformed, reborn of thought
As though a rainbow had crested the tear-soaked sky
For surrounded by death her heart held fast
Her body would succumb, her love would not die.

Her children's touch, their voices such joy
She held it in the folds of her soul
Welling there like a fountain of truth
Heaven's eternity looming gold.

From her I will carry this essence
For I have seen it now firsthand
There is no fear in ending this life
We're going back to where we began.

Born in love, we'll die the same
Leaving love in our wake His command
So be proud and joyous she was yours
For no finer woman has blessed this land.

Remember always what she taught me
Though our encounters were quiet and brief

Love all your life, your family, your friends, smile for heaven awaits
Stand strong and pure, be happy as well, and don't let your spirit give way to grief.

IV

Psalm 51:11 Do not cast me away from Your presence, And do not take Your Holy Spirit from me.

Teacher's Café

The ocean in all its vastness, dwarfing mountain ranges and plunging to immeasurable depths has always been a source of inspiration and solace for me. The crashing surf, the salty mist, knowing that it is the source of wind and climate, acting as the fulcrum in a fragile balance of survival for all living creatures allows me to reflect on the meager circumstance of humanity. Most of us, no matter our self-proclaimed importance or stature, are insignificant to the world. A sobering thought, which on these occasions would leave me to ponder: Where is the value in my life?

My name is John Michael McGee. My wife, Madeleine, and I own a place on the Oregon coast. Where exactly is not important, but what is important is the letter I found coiled into a clear glass bottle that floated ashore at my feet one day. When I first found the letter and the charred bottle that held it, I thought it might be a high school project to chart the tides and currents, or possibly the aching of a broken heart with no where else to turn. Yet as I opened the bottle, pulling the cork that was sealed over with a waxy mantel, I knew its contents would change my life, just as I knew the day our child was born that my journey had gained a greater purpose.

What follows now is the letter as I found it . . .

To whoever finds this letter, may I be your benefactor. For only hindsight sparkles with clarity, and that is all that I have to give.

When I arrived at the edge of the town, I stood in awe of its singular beauty. I could see the vein in every leaf of every tree that lined the street before me, the flesh of their trunks flickering in a golden light. The sky was a ceramic blue as if a perfect teacup had been tipped over the world. How I had come to this place at first was a mystery. I had no recollection of a recent past; just a litany of flashes that defined my history, yet with each step the truth would become clearer as if I was rising through a tent of bubbles to the surface of a crystalline lake.

This small town, which had no name I can recall, was much like the village in Vermont where my grandparents had lived when I was a child. Bungalows of white and blue and green stood back from the curb with friendly yards, the sprinklers of some casting out rainbows in the midday sun. I began to walk toward what seemed in my mind as the center of town, although I did not know or care if I was strolling north or south, only sensing I was going the right direction, as though a migratory bird would make his journey without thought.

A knot of people stood at the corner as I approached, unnoticing at first, then welcoming me with a unified smile.

"Good day to you, sir," a dark-haired man said. "You look as though you have traveled far."

"Frankly, I do not know how far I have come."

"Not unusual. Could I be of help? Are you hungry?"

"I guess -- I guess I am -- hungry."

He put his hand on my shoulder and led me around the corner. "Then you must eat. My name is Simon. Let me show you a wonderful place to be nourished."

Nourished? I found his choice of words odd, yet I immediately felt a comfort in his touch, not unlike my father's when he was still alive.

It was only a short distance until I saw the sign that hung above the sidewalk showing the entrance to Teachers Café. The day was bright with a natural light that electrified all the colors in my sight. Yet it was such a gentle light, soft, that I ruminated over the idea that I could see so well, yet I needed no sunglass to sooth my eyes. Simon led me inside and guided me to a stool at the counter just as a man burst through the saloon doors that led to the kitchen.

"Teach," Simon said. "I have a customer for you. He's hungry, and I knew you would be just the ticket to conquer his appetite. Though he is a little confused at the surroundings."

"So it would seem," Teach replied.

Simon left with a pat to my back, and I sat wondering how he knew of my confusion, my chin resting in the web of my hand.

"So what would you like?" Teach asked.

The question caught my attention. As though but a moment had passed, I wanted to thank Simon, yet as I turned, I realized he was already gone from sight. Teachers Café was full of customers. I never noticed customers on the way in, and now I could feel apprehension pulling taut the ropes of my stomach. Nothing seemed as it should be: the air was too fresh, the day too clear, and all the people in the café looked too familiar. The only person who appeared to be a stranger was Teach.

My mind started to reel: Had I been drugged? The euphoria I was feeling could only be induced from some sort of drug, I surmised. Paranoia was a side effect of some powerful hallucinogens, I knew. That had to be what was happening. As long as I went along, the euphoria was ever present. Only when I questioned my situation came the hint of paranoia.

"So, son, are you hungry, or are you just going to sit there with your mouth open like a baby bird waiting for his mother?" Teach asked.

"Sorry, I'm just trying to get my bearings."

"Not unusual, "he replied. "I have a chicken-fried steak special today. You want that?"

I nodded my head and started searching my arms for needle marks. Curiously, I didn't find any, not a blemish, and the scar on my forearm from the car wreck in 1984 was gone. Vanished without a trace. The paranoia was back. I took a deep breath and gathered my thoughts. What I was sensing had to be a dream. It wasn't real. I was dreaming. I took another deep breath and released a fist of tension. Okay, sit back and go along, I told myself. There was nothing to be afraid of. In fact as dreams go, what I was encountering was not a nightmare, but probably the most pleasant illusion I had ever had.

Teach set a plate of food in front of me. Chicken fried steak, a baked sweet potato, corn on the cob -- it was one of my favorite meals.

"Something to drink?"

"Yes. Water please."

Teach left, returning with a pitcher in his hand. "All in all you've had a pretty good life, wouldn't you say, friend?" He filled a glass in front of me with water and moved a napkin within my reach.

I had a mouth full of sweet potato, the taste superb. "A good life? Yes," I said finally after clearing my throat. "Of course, I have made a lot of good choices."

"How so?"

"Well, my father wanted me to take over the café. Come to think of it, it looked a lot like yours."

"Really," he said with a quizzical air.

"Yeah, " I said pausing, my sight arcing over my shoulder. "But I decided to go to college and get my degree. I've spent the last twenty-five years in private practice. I'm a doctor."

"How interesting."

"I know," I said raising a palm like a stop sign. "First thing people think is: 'He went into it for the money.' But really I just wanted to help people. The money was a gift."

"You've been very fortunate. The majority of people don't have the drive, or the opportunities for that matter, to pursue medicine."

"It's a tough road all right, but I overcame it."

"By the way, how is Madeleine?" he asked.

"My wife?" I stared at him, tried to see a wrinkle in his face that would let the dream come through. "She's fine," I said.

"Wonderful family. A boy, a girl -- pretty much the American dream."

"Well, it isn't easy, but I have always been a faithful and dedicated father."

"Never any thoughts of roaming," Teach grinned. "I mean there are plenty of opportunities to stray."

"Well," I chuckled. "I'm no different than anyone else, but my philosophy has always been: Once you're married you can look . . . okay, maybe let your mind wander on the dark side a bit . . . but don't touch. It just costs too much in the long run."

"Yes, money is important."

"It's not just the money," I said adamantly. "I mean I wouldn't want to hurt Madeleine . . . or the kids." I took a bite of chicken fried steak. "I mean, I like money, don't get me wrong, but I don't believe all that crap that 'money is the root of all evil.' "

Teach winked. "I think it's actually stated, 'The love of money is the root of all evil.' "

"Whatever. I don't see anything wrong with having it."

"I don't either," he said. "Besides you look like a generous guy."

"I give my fair share. I mean taxes -- well no one gets a kick out of paying taxes. I do give money to United Way every year." I chuckled to myself. "Besides it is easier to get them off the phone when you just shell out a few bucks and get it over with."

Teach moved off down the counter and rang up a donut and coffee. He was a tall man, stately, with nice eyes. His hair was in a ponytail. I tore my way through the corn on the cob and was just wiping the butter from my chin when he returned.

"Sounds like you played by all the rules. Any regrets?"

"You mean about the past?"

"It has occurred to me that one can't get to the future without examining the past."

"I suppose you have a point." I thought about the past for a moment, and then answered, "No, I don't have any regrets. I'm a good man by all standards I think. I mean I don't cheat or steal, and I never murdered anybody or committed adultery. I helped my parents, may God bless them, until the day they died. My kids have successful careers, and they nor Madeleine have never lacked for anything."

"Strange choice of words," he replied.

"In what way?"

"Oh, I just mean you don't seem like the 'prayerful' type. 'May God bless them' I think you said."

I thought about the remark, trying to justify my statement. However, I never really did go in for prayers. "True," I said at length. "I was always told God helps those who help themselves. You have to count on yourself first. I don't think God gets involved in the everyday of people's lives."

Teach seemed puzzled. "What does He get involved in?"

"Well, I guess, when you die you have to fill him in on your life, and he makes a judgment as to your acceptability for heaven. But if you're a good person, no worries right?"

"Sort of a Buddhist mentality wouldn't you think?"

"Call it what you want. I just feel you can find God anywhere. Like walk out in a forest. Or look at the ocean. If God isn't a part of all that ... I mean somebody had to set off the firecracker that put the universe into motion."

"Good point."

"I just don't think you have to be crawling to God every five minutes with your every need. It's ludicrous actually, to think he would have the time, or the capacity to deal with all of us at that level. I am sure he has plenty of real problems to worry about besides people like me."

Teach smiled and began wiping down the counter.

"Just between you and me," I said. "Churches are a racket. It's just a business like owning a hardware store. You advertise, and people come in and buy what they want. I'm just not buying a lot of what they're selling. Heck, look at the Catholic Church for instance. That's where I was raised. They have more rituals than a juju woman -- it's mostly man-made stuff, by the way. No, if I need to pray, all I need to do is walk out into a forest and think about it."

"You spend a lot of time in the forest? I thought you were a doctor."

"You know what I mean. If I need God, I know where I can find Him."

"Would you like any dessert -- maybe some coffee to wash that down?"

"No, actually, I feel pretty good. I don't know if it was the food, or the conversation . . ." I gazed out the café window. "Or the surroundings, but I feel pretty content at the moment."

"Nourishment is my specialty."

I started to get up from my stool as if I had somewhere to go. "So what do I owe you?"

"Everything," he replied.

I hesitated. "No really. How much was it?"

"Forget it. It was on the house. Besides, there's no way you can pay me for it anyway."

I searched my pocket. "You're right. I'm broke. I don't even have a credit card." What a dream, I thought, but how was it going to end? I didn't feel threatened and there certainly wasn't anything erotic about Teach or the food. This was the craziest dream I had ever been in.

"So are you ready?"

Suddenly Simon was standing in front of me.

My Father's House

"Simon? Where did you come from?"

"I've got the car."

I looked around and Teach was gone. Teach, all the people -- poof! -- evaporated into thin air. Suddenly, I was sitting in the back of a 1955 Cadillac, black with button-tuck leather seats.

I succumbed to the moment. "Okay, so where are we headed?"

"Edge of town. From there you'll be on your own."

I gazed out my window. Look at all these spectacular trees, I thought to myself. The bungalows were gone; just trees remained. A smile found its way to my mouth, and I giggled silently, for in my mind I could hear Teach's words, "Everything." What did he mean by that? And for a moment, a brief jostling of my spirit, I was overcome with the sensation of Hope. Hope for my family.

But my smile eroded, and a lonely sigh left my lips. Like a guilty slap in the face, as Simon drove away from downtown, I realized that his car had no handles on the inside. A piece of Plexiglas separated him and me, and I was trapped in the backseat. It was hot, steamy, as if the heater on and I was somewhere in South Carolina or Georgia. An ice cube ran down my spine. I twisted in my seat, all at once uncomfortable. The air was getting hard to breathe. A thought provoked me: Trees . . . a forest. I'm in a forest. But that would mean . . .

I turned, putting a knee up on the cushion, and with the palm of my hand, wiped a hole in the accumulating breath on the rear window. A small hole, but through it, all things became clear. The bright light that was once Teacher's Café was fading fast in the expanding distance. Above me, ominous clouds were poised in the sky, swirling down behind the car like smoke from an oil fire. A flock of birds raced inland seeking shelter. The trees, once green with foliage, were now scorched, standing like silent sentinels of disaster along the road. I slipped down in my seat, my muscles suddenly heavy; my heart now just an echo unto itself.

In the front seat, Simon had disappeared, replaced by a man with a nose that looked phallic and obscene. I remembered church as a child being this quiet . . . except the man in the front seat was gnashing his teeth, and the sound was growing louder and louder and louder.

Minutes later, the car turned onto a gravel road. Rocks cracked against the floorboards. I sat up straight and gripped the edge of the seat with my hands.

"Who was that man?" I cried. "Teach, who was he?"

The man in the front seat snickered. I could smell his foul breath, his body rife with the stench of dead animals. "Jesus, my friend. That was Jesus." Then he laughed a roiling laugh that erupted boils across my back. "Didn't you know him?" he said. "John Michael McGee -- a man of the forest indeed!"

I tried to hold back, but the boils were searing with pain, and I felt an alkaline tear burn the flesh down my cheek, my eyes red with the blood of my children, my grandchildren and theirs ad infinitum.

I suffer now in a forsaken world, the same one I was deceived into believing was not real. I recognize no one. No one recognizes me. It is vacant and cold of emotion, except anguish that smolders rancid in the hollow of my chest. I will never feel the love of Christ, only the torment of my abusers, here where my name is uttered in whispers as one would a lewd remark.

Forever yours,
John Michael McGee

I still have the letter. I carry it with me everywhere. I cannot explain it, nor will I ever try, for I have learned not to waste my life being too proud or intelligent to test God's ways. My fate may be sealed. Only God knows if I wrote that letter and threw into the River Styx -- it was my signature after all -- but if I can save one soul by knowing of the letter's existence, I will have fulfilled the purpose that was intended.

For me, discovering the letter has refocused my commitments. I see now that the true measure of a man is valued in the only commodity that He cannot, or will not command -- Love. When I fell in love with Madeleine, I wanted to learn everything about her. I adored her. God wants no more from us, or no less. That is why I will spend the rest of my earthly life reaching and seeking for God's hand, so that I will know Him when my day comes. For Heaven will be granted by His grace alone, not by the foolish tally of my good works.

So take heed of the deception that the world would like us to believe; don't wait for a bottle filled with Truth. We are not promised next year, next week, nor even our next breath. When death comes, you will be alone, as I, with no one to rely on, with no science to provide the answers, naked of your accomplishments, traveling a course into another existence, this time for eternity.

Printed in the United States
92584LV00004B/538/A